Requiem

Dominic Cain

BookLeaf
Publishing

India | USA | UK

Presentation by *BookLeaf Publishing*

Web: www.bookleafpub.com

E-mail: info@bookleafpub.com

ISBN: 9789358318920

First edition 2023

Dedicated to my three roses

The first was forsaken

The second was taken

The third stopped my heart from breaking

Genesis

Never a truer thing in the universe
Than the power to share experience through
verse
Each of us is writing a never ending story
In which we hope our legacy will be one of hope
and glory

As the book of life is written the pages become
torn and faded
Every imperfection a reflection of that which has
become so jaded
It's true that life is the most beautiful ride
But it's never easy fighting against the rising tide

We find strength from that which is not strong
In order to combat that which has gone so wrong
We always find a way to learn from the mistakes
that we've made
Sadly though the scars they leave behind never
quite fade

But what do you do when the fabric of your
reality changes overnight
The nature of which is impossible to understand
try as you might

Let me know when to expect the sun to once
again shine
And remind me what it's like to feel what you
might call fine

Pain Redefined

Throughout this lifetime of existence
The world has not left me under false pretense
I have seen suffering and I have seen pain
And felt dark thoughts from which I must refrain

But losing your most loved one elevates pain to
a new dimension
One so deep, that to escape it requires the
highest ascension
Suddenly you feel your entire world stop turning
And each and every fibre of your being begins
burning

However somewhere deep in this emotional
maze
A spark can still be felt reminding us of better
days
Despite every breath without you in the world
feeling torturous
Nothing in this universe happens because its
fortuitous

The road ahead is not without challenge
To forge a new future, pieces of the past we
must scavenge

But you left behind a legacy greater than you
ever could have known
And none of us who remains needs to embark
upon this journey alone

Crystal Child

Two souls eternally intertwined
The meaning of life ultimately defined
Existing views of the world undermined
Before I found you I was blind

For so long I was sabotaging myself
Abusing my soul with no care for my health
But something about you made me want to
believe
And become everything I once dared to achieve

Alone when I drink
Countless thoughts of you do I think
You're everything I didn't know I need
Your kiss has begun writing a book I'm eager to
read

There are no limits to the number of words I can
write about you
And I'll spend the rest of my life doing so, it's
true
You've no idea of how much I truly feel, not the
faintest clue
I beseech the universe to not have you be just
another passer through

Reconciliation

It has been some time since I last picked up the
pen
Plenty of emotions have been felt since then
But my feelings have been raw and
overwhelming
I've been struggling with the consequences they
bring

I tread a fine line between darkness and light
And never once do I feel a moment of respite
I have become a being of pure emotion and
intuition
No longer in my mind does logic come to
fruition

The greatest irony are my champagne problems
Drowning myself in the very elixir I use to solve
them
They say absence makes the heart grow fonder
In my experience it makes the torture go on for
longer

But now I sit glass in hand hoping to reconcile
with my feelings

In order to deal with so many things that have
left my spirit reeling
The first step to this is opening my heart
In order for my feelings to fuel my art

Numb

For so many years now my defences have been
eroded
Deep inside I have become more and more jaded
Tonight I rode home feeling nothing at all
Each day from grace do I fall

I'm tired of feeling loss and regret
How much more do I need to drink in order to
forget
I still haven't accepted the fact that you're gone
Having been called upon to spread love, light
and compassion

Getting through many days can be a chore
And often I ask myself what I'm doing it for
The answer is not always apparent
The world is worse off without your special
talent

Sometimes I cry so much I run out of tears
Waking up in a world without you is one of my
worst fears
But I dig deep to find strength to move forward
I can't let your loss be any more than a foreword

One Way Mirror

I stare at you all through this one way mirror
So close yet so far as I cut a lonely figure
My pain comes from not knowing what I'm
doing wrong
Watching your chaos and disorder unfold whilst
writing this song

The first can argue without warning
Yet they'll be just fine come the morning
Neither of you know just how much you mean to
me
Just know I'll be there before and after you've
taken the knee

The second were fated to meet
Now you've found each other your journeys are
complete
Your personalities fit one another like a glove
You are one of the purest forms of love

The third are a peculiar one
Ever the opposites, it doesn't feel that long since
your tale begun
It warms my heart to see your souls intertwined

In each other eternal happiness is what you have
found

Sometimes I am unsure as to what more I must
learn
As I search the earth for the partner for whom I
yearn
I wonder what separates me from the rest of you
Just the architect of this mirror, that's who

Mr Bottle

Have you met my friend Mr Bottle
I like to talk to him every day
He loves to sit and listen
But he never has much to say

Truth is often I feel quite lonely
Living in a world of 8 billion on my own
So on a night I'd call up Mr Bottle
He's always happy to hear me moan

Mr Bottle was there after I lost my angel
My heart splinters every time I see her face
So my friend Mr Bottle tries his very best
To wrap me once more in her warm embrace

Sadly Mr Bottle can't bring her back
Lord knows he tries his best
So each night after I've shed my last tear
He lays me down to rest

Demerara Sugar

Where once my heart fumbled in the dark
Meeting you ignited the brightest spark
With a happy couple's holy matrimony as our
view
Demerara sugar is where I met you

I quickly lost myself in your ocean blue eyes
While you regaled me with tales of savagery
under sunny skies
Later you'd welcome me into your avenue
Demerara sugar is where I fell for you

A life of love and laughter was soon to follow
Together we worked to build a better tomorrow
That stationary road was the culmination of
everything we'd been through
Demerara sugar was where I flourished with you

But sadly the peace was not to last
With isolation and the winds of change nailing
themselves to our mast
September 26th became a date I eschew
Demerara sugar is where I forsook you

I have never forgiven myself for the future I
stole
Dreams of stately homes and Disneyland with
my toasty cinnamon roll
Now you've moved onto pastures new
Demerara sugar is where my heart floundered
without you

Beresford

Even now there are no words to say
That sum up just how much I miss you
Each lost thought, moment and memory
Is unbearable to subject myself to

I've never forgiven myself for letting you go
I'd go back to my younger self and scream at
him no
I'd beg and plead for him to stop right there
If you throw this love away, your life you don't
deserve to share

I miss you each and every day
I spent so long trying to bury us
I drink to try and make your memory go away
But the resurrection of your presence always
finds a way

I'm finding ways of dealing with negativity
But my regrets of you continue to keep me in
captivity
I miss every part of you so much
From your beautiful eyes to your sweet and
gentle touch

The Strangest Storm

My life is like the strangest storm
Bitterly cold yet tropically warm
Every day for me is like a battle inside
And I know whom not in I can confide

I am fortunate to have received blessings in
excess
All the while my head and heart are a mess
I miss you so bloody much
My family and friends have been a sorely
needed crutch

Imagine being the architect of your success and
demise
Divinely watched over but not always so wise
I strive to be a better man each and every day
But it's hard when no one in life shows you the
way

Some days I laugh out loud whilst others I stare
out over bridges
Occasionally I'm content with just eating cheese
out of fridges
I look at myself in the mirror and think about
what I've done

Do I really need to love myself in order to have
fun

I don't know how to think and feel anymore
When every time I close my eyes at night I see
you walking out of that door
But I'm always working to get my head back on
track
Even if there's nothing I can do to bring you
back

Rosina

This is a poem about a special mother
I'm quite sure she was one like no other
She's taught me every little thing I know
She was like the pot of gold at the end of the
rainbow

Growing up I couldn't have asked for more
support
Mum knows best is what I always thought
I know I could always have a cry on your
shoulder
And ask for your advice as I got older

Thanks to you I have some clue of what to do
And I'm prepared to deal with anything new
No matter what I'm always here for you
I'll support you with anything you're going
through

These past few years have been tough
With many moments that were more than a little
rough
Like a phoenix you always found a way to rise
from ashes
Love and light radiated off you in bright flashes

Every day you inspire me to be a better man
You offered support and guidance in ways that
no one else can
I'm so proud of everything you were able to do
Words cannot describe the entirety of my love
for you

Crossing Paths

Often before my bedtime
I have found myself inspired to write a little
rhyme
About unexpectedly finding myself lost in a rose
tinted haze
Forever grateful that our paths have crossed
ways

She inspires me to be my best man
And challenge myself to do more than I ever
thought I can
I draw inspiration from her inner strength
To support her I'd go to an infinite length

I can open up to her completely to her
My feelings clear as Cornish water
Never did I think I'd meet someone like you
When someone asks me who my favourite
person is, it's you I point to

It's a privilege to ride this wave of change
together
Your insight into life makes it all the more
fresher
I can't wait for us to explore this world

And observe how the next chapters of our lives
are unfurled

Devotion

I wish upon you an abundance of love and light
As you sleep soundly in your bed tonight
Talking to you always makes me feel just right
You always motivate me to reach a greater
height

My favourite thing in the world is waking up
next to you
Your warmth and grace makes that true
My heart and soul spills out in the midst of this
haze
I could describe my feelings for you in so many
ways

When I wake you're the first thing I think of
Everything about you I love
You're the last thing I think of when I fall asleep
Your company is so precious to me to keep

I forever count down the hours until I get to see
you again
For you I'd ride the longest train
It's impossible to explain how you make things
feel so right

The universe with you in it is infinitely more bright

Nightingale

Imagine meeting someone so special
They change the composition of your universe
So important and majestic
For them you write verse after verse

Each day passed is a day closer to having you in
my arms
You can't imagine how seduced I am by your
charms
No written or spoken word can truly express
what you mean to me my nightingale
And no worldly action describes how important
you are to my tale

Though I don't smile all the time
The very thought of you inspires me to rhyme
Because I want you more than anything
And your affection is what I crave you bring

Whether they're asleep or awake you wish them
well
The entirety of your feelings for them you wish
you could tell
Good night my incredible angel
I pray you sleep deeply and well

Impossible

Though it's been easy to feel for my nightingale
And in turn use that energy to compose many a
tale
The truth is that these feelings are not always
sunshine and rainbows
The truest extent of what goes on in my head no
one knows

I am enticed by your boundless creativity
And enthralled by your endless energy
The world is so much more fun with you around
When I'm with you I sprout wings and fly off
the ground

But sometimes I wonder if it's possible to build
something with you
Maybe us wanting the same thing from life is
not so true
Not only that but I deeply desire warmth, taste
and touch
But lately of that there's not been that much

No matter what happens I crave your presence in
my life

Without you my mind would have fallen victim
to endless strife
But maybe the love I thought we could one day
have is impossible
I hope the conclusion I'm reaching is not too
improbable

Proud

To say I'm proud of your accomplishments is an
understatement
I'm happy to stand back and observe your hard
work in amazement
From such a young age you demonstrated
incredible ambition
It didn't take you long for the vehicle of your
dreams to fire up it's ignition

You started from the bottom and learnt
everything you could
You approached things diligently and did
everything you should
Now you're reaping the rewards of all your hard
work
Years of knowledge and study now just like
clockwork

You embody her passion, fire and determination
Her desire to succeed and go beyond any
perceived limitation
I know she will be looking down delighted for
your success
Not only your career but the rest of your heart
and soul she will forever bless

But amidst all this progress and promotion
You must remember to keep an eye on your
emotion
To ensure you balance work and play
In order to ensure you feel your best each day

Lonestar

As I look back on the twists and turns of life
A common occurrence has always held to my
neck the sharpest knife
No matter where I was or with whom
I have always felt like the only person in the
room

That's not to say I lack companionship
Indeed I am inundated with beautiful friendship
I am surrounded by the most loving kinsfolk
Who's love wraps around me like a warm cloak

But despite all that I feel like deep down I'm not
quite understood
The very foundations of how our society works
have begun to draw metaphorical blood
The only person who could understand these
words that I'm saying
Is the same person for whom I lie awake each
night praying

With each passing day I feel my proximity to
society grow ever more far
And increasingly I identify as an eccentric
lonestar

Logic and reason are becoming meaningless to
me
Operating on raw emotion now is helping me to
be free

Verse

I was never one for poetry in my younger years
I never appreciated its power to convey love and
fears
But now I can't imagine not being able to write
song and verse
My emotional instability, it helps to disperse

Once she asked me how to write poetry
And honestly for me it's as easy as planting a
tree
But I'm not sure how to explain where my
words come from
I just zero in on what I'm feeling at that moment
and beat it like a drum

I have always been one for a healthy dose of
flair
And I know exactly from whom that's come
from and where
This universe we live in is pure energy
If you can harness it's rhythm then you and your
words can dance in synergy

My verse may not always make sense

But the beauty is that I make no claim of written
pretence
I close my eyes and let my soul imprint itself on
the page
Almost like the words are written by an
otherworldly sage

www.ingramcontent.com/pod-product-compliance
Lightning Source LLC
La Vergne TN
LVHW051245200726
843510LV00011B/1700